Permission to Breathe

For my sister Suki and my brother Tim

Previous publications
Cloves of Garlic (Smith/Doorstop Books 1989)
Thinking of Happiness (Peterloo Poets 1991)
    (Poetry Book Society Recommendation)
In The Fruit Cage (Smith/Doorstop Books 1997)
The Tightrope Wedding (Smith/Doorstop Books 1999)
    (Poetry Book Society Recommendation)

Acknowledgements
Thanks are due to the editors of the following publications in which some of these poems first appeared: *Areté, London Magazine, The North, Other Poetry, Penniless Press, Pitch, Poetry London, Poetry Review, The Rialto, The Shop, Smoke, Soundings, Times Literary Supplement.*

Permission to Breathe

Michael Laskey

Smith/Doorstop Books

Published 2004 by
Smith/Doorstop Books
The Poetry Business
The Studio
Byram Arcade
Westgate
Huddersfield HD1 1ND

Copyright © Michael Laskey 2004
All Rights Reserved

ISBN 1-902382-61-7

Michael Laskey hereby asserts his moral right to be identified as the author of this book.

British Library Cataloguing-in-Publication Data. A catalogue record for this book is available from the British Library.

Typeset at The Poetry Business
Printed by Peepal Tree Press, Leeds
Cover picture 'Diver' © Pris Forrest (charcoal on paper)
Author's photograph © Claire McNamee

Distributed by Central Books Ltd., 99 Wallis Road, London E9 5LN

The Poetry Business is a member of Inpress (Independent Presses Representation): www.inpressbooks.co.uk.

The Poetry Business gratefully acknowledges the help of Arts Council England and Kirklees Cultural Services.

CONTENTS

7	The Corpse
8	The Barrow
9	The New Car
10	The Machine
11	Freehold
12	Stanislaw's Iron
13	The Surrender at Somosierra Pass, 1936
14	Fear
15	Joining the M25
16	Seeing You Off
17	The Scar
18	On My Birthday
19	The List
20	A Breath of Fresh Air
21	Afterlife
22	Resurrection
23	Getting Warm
24	On the Phone
26	Norm Watson Auction
27	Karen and Melvin, Wedding Dance, Meadowbrook Hall, Alberta
28	Kelly Frank
29	Why
30	Crabbing
32	The One
33	Little Sister
34	A Chance
35	Rereading
36	Nobody

37	Rain
38	The Show
39	The Marina
40	The Flat-warming
41	Thirst
42	Creeks
43	In the Aboriginal Cultures Gallery, Adelaide
44	Near Williamstown, South Australia
45	Living the Silence
46	Awkward Things
47	Take Two
48	On His Own
49	This Morning
50	Past Talking
51	Visitors
52	Lapse
53	Identity Parade
54	Old School Tie
55	Travelling with St Thèrese
56	A Meeting
57	Close
58	Mending a Puncture
59	Permission to Breathe
60	Old Money
61	The Pain on His Face
62	Getting On
63	The Lawnmower

The Corpse

He shares my morning cup of tea, likes it
colder than me. Staring at the empty
blue window, he's my dad propped up
glimpsed again through the ward's swing doors.

I reach for my book, find my place
or jump up quick, wash, give myself
a close shave, inhale soap, and froth
the strong teeth he bares at the mirror.

He's a rude child. I rattle him off
downstairs, stop his mouth with muesli,
fresh fruit. Once I'd kiss him at the school
gates and get on with my life.

But he grows so fast. No time since
he was nothing but a blink in my eye,
a blank at the end of my tunnel,
yet self-evident now, so conspicuous

in the tube some woman stands up
and offers me her seat. Though my feet
are killing me, I decline, my smile
tightened by his grin. He knows me

inside out. He's like a parent
come to collect me from a party
I've just started to enjoy. Ridiculously
punctual. *Oh, he can wait.* Yes, he can wait.

And he does, exchanging ghastly
benign glances with that corpse
of yours at the way we fret
over deadlines or how badly we've slept.

Kelly Frank

Behind him the fence and then nothing
but prairie for a thousand miles
and skies so incredibly riddled
with stars you look closer and see
the window frame, realise they're nails
holding what must have been red
tarpaper – mock brick – in place
on the side of a house or a shed.

And it's plain now the boy has his back
to the wall, his shirt stained with grease,
pocket half torn off, cuffs flapping
and a safety-pin for the missing
top button. Hand hooked on the wire.
A sore in the corner of his mouth.
Yet expectant, lips parted, his fair
skin mapping a galaxy of freckles.

The New Car

Coming in with a bag of windfall Bramleys
I touch the cool wing of the car
with the back of my hand. Its whiteness
through the window still lightens each morning.
It's the comfort I drive in, no longer
tensing at any tremor in the engine,
suspicious of each odd rattle or knock.
It's what he's become: a weight off my mind,
a Rover, just like he used to drive,
only bigger. I'm cutting the bruised bits
out of the apples, adding sugar; telling
myself I'm sure he'd approve.

The Machine

In the daytime it lived on the window ledge
at the end of the kitchen, plugged in
beside the dark brown two pint jug
he kept topped up. After taking his pills
each morning while he waited for her
to come down for breakfast, he tipped
the night's ropy mixture of mucus
and water down the sink and rinsed
the tank and the clear plastic tubing
under the hot tap intently,
scoured the nozzle with a fine bottle-brush.

For four years he nursed it, monitored
its puttering engine. Unflinching
he sucked up the phlegm bubbling out
at her stoma, he smiled as he caught it,
he passed her a Kleenex, the ointment.
For four years he stayed alive
and breathed for her. She was my mother
and he – remember it, remember
how I even corrected the Registrar
of Births and Deaths, put her right
punctiliously when she called him my father.

Freehold

When the house finally went
over the cliff, it was almost
a relief – we'd already grieved
for our ceiling rose in the playroom
and given up on the garden.
Later the longshore drift
would float off wonky rafts
of floorboards and joists, all trace
of our precious sash window frames.

Big winds behind spring tides
and the beach resurfaced,
a clean sweep of shingle.
Except for this: not what
it looked like, a mill chimney,
but a well shaft, capped,
its blackened bricks mortared
and perfectly stacked. A well
we hadn't even known we owned.

Stanislaw's Iron

It was while he was stuck in Luebeck
in the DP camp after the war
that he found it, poking about
in a burnt out house. He liked
its coldness, its clang, the swung
weight of it snug in his fist.
But in the hut Tadeusz heated it up
on the stove and they learnt how to press
creases back into their trousers
and put a brave face on those shirts.

With precious few belongings it went
in the dark with him on the boat
to Australia. It kept its counsel
in hostels, bunkhouses, shacks;
survived incomprehension, translation,
loss of function, an Aussie wife
wedded to the electric future;
and it outlived Stanislaw himself
to stand on the shelf of this poem –
matt black, solid, due for a dust.

The Surrender at Somosierra Pass, 1936

A photo he kept:
seven of them stumbling
among the dead
down the slope,
flanked and outnumbered
by nationalist troops
rifles at the ready.

A photo he kept
to remember how
they'd thrown down their own
assortment of guns,
as they scrambled out
from the cover of the rocks,
raising their hands.

A photo he kept
not to forget
the way they'd stretched them
abjectly high,
drained of defiance,
only not
wanting to die.

Fear

Fear of not waking up
Fear of the rats in the compost heap, iron teeth and the flicker
                        of a gristly tail
Fear of the postman's tread on the gravel, that handwriting,
                        envelopes like this
Fear of remembering
Fear of forgetting
    of Henry in hospital, propped up, chewing his stew,
                      no recognition in his eyes
Fear of water shortages, overpopulation
    of the mob surging up your alley looking for Cinna
Fear of the news
    of the same old thoughts in your head washing back and forth
Fear of the sea
    of the live thing underfoot or brushing your forearm as you swim
    of the swans nesting by the path beside the Mere
Fear of the frightened man
    of your first headmaster's disapproval, your dead father's anger
Fear of drinking from her porcelain tea cups
Fear of the axe-head you still haven't fixed
Fear of the articulated lorry's grille huge in the rear-view mirror
    of fog, of black ice
    of the phone ringing in the small hours
    of the children dying before you
Fear of light years, what might fall from the sky
Fear of utter subterranean darkness
Fear of embarrassment
    of bogs, of sinking under your own weight
Fear of a right-sided stroke
    of the tyranny of patient nurses
    of dying and not being able to die
Fear of waking up

Joining the M25

It was on the A12 going south
beyond Chelmsford last March.
He was stuck in a slow-moving stream
of traffic in the outside lane
on another visit to his mother
in hospital after her latest
operation, when it suddenly came
to him that he wouldn't mind dying.

He could indicate left and pull over
into a lay-by, turn off
the engine, the World at One,
and simply stop driving
air in and out of his lungs.
The children were grown, there was nothing
vital he'd be leaving undone.

Surprised, he drove steadily on,
only gathering necessary speed
as he joined the M25,
feeling lighter somehow, relieved.

Seeing You Off

Though red double deckers are parked
in all but one of the bays in both dark
green corrugated iron hangars,
the depot's deserted – no-one else
waiting, the brick office locked, mugs left
on the draining board below a backfiring
Ascot like ours at Southborough Road,
small print health and safety regulations
pinned up behind a metal desk
with a calendar pad showing time stopped
last Wednesday, and hanging from a peg
a baseball cap, a lady's red umbrella.
Lost property. I check the framed
timetable and try to have faith, keep
chatting, read you the signs – *Buses
reversing. Danger: Asbestos roof
will not bear walking upon.* You try
for a smile. We could do with a seat.
I point out the ragwort flowering
between slack wire and concrete posts.
But suddenly the bus is here, changing down
under the railway bridge, an 84,
shuddering, blocking out the sunlight,
and now it's come and I'm helping you on
I don't want you to go, to let go
of my arm, though there's plenty of room
and some of them I recognise – 'El Cid'
rising up in the aisle and there's Gran
with an eager man, surely your dad,
and at the back isn't that Uncle Tony
waving one of his foul menthol cigarettes?

The Scar

What were they playing, *it* or something?
Glancing behind him as he dashed
down the street he'd skidded on gravel
in the gutter and come a cropper.
At the sight of the blood, his flayed
knee, his screams filled the world.

She grimaced at the wound but went on
sponging and dabbing it, shushing him,
washing out the grit till he sensed
her calm and knew that it wasn't
too bad though it hurt, and that Dettol
did really sting like she warned him.

These mornings waking up in the dark
he sees her die, sees how the blood
drains from her face
and wishes again that he'd stood
by her hospital bed the last time
she came round and somehow not cried.

On My Birthday

Sun; and lunch out with Kay and Tim –
smoked squid and a glass of house white;
a morning and an afternoon swim;
some raspberry picking; and filming
for a poem in the evening with Jack,
the ease and the interest of that.
New books, a brown teapot, a slop –
any number of touching presents,
but none less looked for, more precious
than yours, these tears welling up
again, numb months since you died.

The List

Leafing back through my drafts for a spark
of life I come on the list
of questions we wrote out to ask
the doctor that morning. It's a shock
to be there on Elstead Ward
at her bedside again, locked on
to her uncertain breathing, worried
by the blood in the catheter bag
and the lax left side of her face,
not knowing how long she could last
or whether it's really for us,
the sedation we're arguing for
in the corridor – though she's unconscious.
We just can't be sure, it's a matter
of waiting mainly, Dr Clarius
tells us in almost perfect
English. I nod, add his name
to the list on the pad that I'll later
assume was a stab at a poem.

A Breath of Fresh Air

but we couldn't think where –
the car in gear already
at the gate not knowing which way
to turn – when you said *What about
Dolpa's walk?* and I knew at once
where you meant, though we'd never
called it after her before,
she couldn't have done it more
than half a dozen times, that short
stretch of the coastal path
from the caravan park to Ness House
or perhaps not so far, turning back
at the steps to the beach, if she felt
the wind through her cherry red coat.
So I indicate left, change up
as she strikes off the path ahead
through the bracken for an unimpeded
view from the cliff-top, a deep
rapturous breath of sea air
and she lightens, fades away, leaves us
her nickname behind, caught
on these brambles and prickles of gorse.

Afterlife

With the east wind clacking the cat flap
and the breakfast things washed up and stacked
on the drainer, I turn to what's left
of the chicken under foil in the fridge,
set a bowl for the meat on the worktop
and beside it my pan, the deep one,
for the bones – three litres – and begin
on the breast, lumps and strips, lick my fingers,
wrench a leg off, a wing, unpeel
wrinkled skin and add it to the pot
with the gristle, a tendon's white ribbon,
the hinges of the carcass that I snap
and pull apart so the whole thing fits,
the jelly from the plate scraped on top.

Not what he'd have called stock. He kept
an old saw in his kitchen to rip
through to the marrow. It's a thought
that rises to the surface, a bobbing
pearl of fat about to dissolve
in the soup I'm making: a thick
leek and potato, and later
in the week, if it stays this cold
and miserable, lentil and fennel.

Resurrection

You were dead already, I think,
that afternoon, coming and going
quietly, bringing us cups
from the hall to wash up and a stray
glass or two sticky with dregs.

Now we're dead as well, we leave
the crockery draining and climb
our stairs for the last time
to lie at length in the bath
past thought, past hurt, only brought

back to life by the growing cold.

Getting Warm

Just back from a swim they're sitting
over breakfast in the garden getting warm
in the sunshine which picks out the pair
of honeyed wicker chairs, the oak table.
They've plunged the cafetière and drained it,
laid down their spoons in their bowls
and already the bits of core
from the Braeburn they've shared are going
brown and the pared peel's curling more
as it dries. They've fallen silent,
eyes held by the trees at the end
of the garden – may, chestnut and ash
leaves shimmering, shivering, beginning
to turn, to whirl, one's landed
in the cup of her lap. They're entranced,
would never choose to move again,
though clouds accumulate, rain
specks their faces, though snowflakes
settle on their hair and shoulders
and now at their feet a trench opens –
it's a yellow JCB, a pallet
of breeze blocks, brick walls going up
with gaps for the windows, eye-sockets
they stare through blankly, or would
if it wasn't for the ringing of the phone
behind them. He rises stiffly. She leans
forward, stacks things on the tray.

On the Phone

I'm reading a poem, I'm lifting
my morning cup of coffee, trickling
seeds into a drill, perhaps keeping
still not to startle a thought
landed on the curtain that may
be a skipper if it opens its wings,
or at last I'm making a start
on my marking, when they ring.

There's no escape, no defence:
it's Zenith windows again
or Max from Powergen promising
5% off the phone bill.

But who can ignore its ringing?
Not me, despite its reminders
I'm just a wrong number, not
the Co-op at all, I'm sorry.

But for now it's asleep in its cradle.
Tiptoe past. Don't look. Ssh.

Only home an hour and already
Jack's back on the phone – laughter
behind the old playroom door.
In London or Leeds someone's breezing
down the street on their mobile, smiling.

And suddenly see it, feel
the frown I've become, how I sigh
whenever it rings, put off
calling anyone, even Suki.

CONTENTS

7	The Corpse
8	The Barrow
9	The New Car
10	The Machine
11	Freehold
12	Stanislaw's Iron
13	The Surrender at Somosierra Pass, 1936
14	Fear
15	Joining the M25
16	Seeing You Off
17	The Scar
18	On My Birthday
19	The List
20	A Breath of Fresh Air
21	Afterlife
22	Resurrection
23	Getting Warm
24	On the Phone
26	Norm Watson Auction
27	Karen and Melvin, Wedding Dance, Meadowbrook Hall, Alberta
28	Kelly Frank
29	Why
30	Crabbing
32	The One
33	Little Sister
34	A Chance
35	Rereading
36	Nobody

Norm Watson Auction

Forty, fifty people, a quarter of Hussar's
population are crowding Norm Watson's yard
this morning, so many you can hardly see
the stuff stacked in lots they've been sizing up
and can only imagine what else there might be
from the look of the truncated chairs on the left,
the wardrobe, the bedstead leant against
the wall of the house. These are Norm's neighbours
weighing up his personal effects
for anything that could come in handy
or takes their fancy. Friends of his paying
their last respects, trying not to catch
the auctioneer's eye. So what am I
bid for these hats? Who'll start me off?

Karen and Melvin, Wedding Dance,
Meadowbrook Hall, Alberta

There's nothing here, only a crossroads,
a field for the cars and the hall
serving a few hundred people
scattered among hamlets and farms.
So they're glad to be guests. It's their pick-up,
with their present, bow-tied, on the bonnet.
The bottle of Pilsner he's holding
lightly parallels Karen, his wife –
it's as straight and as full – and it matches
him too, his clean open-necked shirt.
As he leans on his elbow the sleeve
of his upper arm may well be brushing
hers. Such a touching young couple,
smiles so composed set against
blank prairie, two fence posts, a strand
of barbed wire and the front of the truck
speckled with countless small deaths.

Kelly Frank

Behind him the fence and then nothing
but prairie for a thousand miles
and skies so incredibly riddled
with stars you look closer and see
the window frame, realise they're nails
holding what must have been red
tarpaper – mock brick – in place
on the side of a house or a shed.

And it's plain now the boy has his back
to the wall, his shirt stained with grease,
pocket half torn off, cuffs flapping
and a safety-pin for the missing
top button. Hand hooked on the wire.
A sore in the corner of his mouth.
Yet expectant, lips parted, his fair
skin mapping a galaxy of freckles.

Why

Because it was incredible
Because you were probably imagining things
Because you'd heard they were moving
Because people do get hysterical
Because you're always positive, it's the way you're made
Because it wasn't your job to deal with complaints like that
Because you've got to get along with the neighbours
Because you swore you'd never turn into your father
Because you have insight, you were convinced he had potential
Because you trusted him
Because you were used to him, he'd been like that for years
Because you didn't like to pry
Because why upset him, he hadn't been any trouble for some time
Because you prefer not to make a fuss
Because it could have been embarrassing
Because he wasn't your responsibility actually
Because you're a taxpayer
Because that evening you had toothache
Because it had been a long old day and you'd only just picked up
                                          your book
Because you've always been a sound sleeper

Crabbing

At the Woomera Detention Centre,
in the January heat, the protest
is growing, more boat people desperate
for their applications to be processed
have sewn their lips together.
A month into your trip, in the cool
of this house with its thick stone walls
in the Adelaide Hills, the remote
in the palm of your hand, you switch off –
another country, but the same
old tricks of due process, inertia,
you catch your mind turning away,
drifting, murky, till it clears
and you find yourself back with the boys,
tuned in to their unbroken voices,
dangling a line tied with laces
of bacon rind over the side
of a quay or next to a pile
on a lopsided jetty. You pay
it out till you feel the weight
touch bottom and let it settle –
not long though, count slowly
to ten – then hoist the bait clear
of the water and check. Chances are
there'll be one or two gripping on,
too avidly feeding to notice
air going past, but easy
does it, hand over hand,
till you've raised them up over the lip
of the bucket and can shake them off,
watch how they slide to the bottom
and jostle the others, so many
thumbnails among them, the boys

keep losing count. The wind freshens,
clouds thicken, but the afternoon's built
around them, it's a shell they fill
so entirely they don't feel the cold
or care about anything more
than this crab that's spilt at their feet
and squares up to them, raised claws hinged
wide open. So brave they must laugh,
dare themselves to dart in and grab it
from behind and add it to the catch.
Later there'll be races: remember
the upended heap unscrambling
on the quay, always one or two left
behind unmoving, but the boys are whooping
as the rest scuttle sideways and drop
back into the clouded water.

The One

After all these years
he turns up
in his new blazer
with the grey piping,
smiling just a little
anxiously, my baby
brother they expected me
to look after. *Peter,
wait* he calls out.
And shaking, shaken,
I round on him:
*I haven't gone.
You're the one
who got drowned
and turned me
into their only child.*

Little Sister

She agreed to be buried, pleased
to be needed, alert to his interest
flagging, his casual glances
at the beach-huts over her shoulder.

She helped dig the hole as well
as she could, though as it grew damp
his metal spade made her new
plastic one feel silly.

She lay down when he said, stretched out,
placed her hands at her sides palms down
and stayed still, only lifting her head
to admire her legs disappearing.

It was cool at first underneath,
then cold. The sand he heaped
on her tummy and chest tickled
as he spread it, patted it flat

and he yelled at her not to breathe
so much, not to giggle, it cracked
the sarcophagus and made her blue
puckered costume show through.

In their album though it's her big front
teeth grinning out, and he's nothing
but a spade dangling, two skinny legs
chopped off just above the knee.

A Chance

in his lunch-hour to nip
to the toyshop on Bliss Street –
it was racing up, Amy's
half-birthday – so the cheers
and was it singing he heard
as he cut down Rose Passage
for a nano-second he imagined
were for her, though as he drew nearer
to the Broadway the noise grew
confused by whistles and jeers
and emerging beside the Prudential
he found the road blocked by the press
of heated protesters pushing
wheelchairs and prams, a brass band,
two orange-robed monks and a phalanx
of nuns or maybe transvestites
flanked by circumspect policemen
heading east towards City Hall
and back out of sight past the gates
of Concordia Park. Could he
somehow slip across, worm through
without being carried away
with the banners, the chanting, the righteous
anger, the prickle of danger?
Leave him on the pavement. You
and I can't make up his mind.

Rereading

Dickens for instance
would be something,
Little Dorrit, I'd start with,
a larderful of language,
but for now make do
with the cereal packet:
my choice of three
exclusive designs
of a snack tray in tough
easy clean melamine,
apparently still
dishwasher safe.

Nobody

If you can't bring yourself to build
a snowman or even to clench
a snowball or two to fling
at the pine tree trunk, at least
find some reason to take you out

of yourself: scrape a patch of grass clear
for the birds maybe; prod at your shrubs
so they shake off the weight, straighten up;
or just stump about leaving prints
of your boots, your breath steaming out.

Promise. Don't let yourself in
for this moment again: the end
of the afternoon, drawing the curtains
on the glare of the garden, a whole
day of snow nobody's trodden.

Rain

So much rain, such a cloudburst, and the downpour
going on so long that the children
won't be fobbed off, they clamour
for their boots and cagoules, they jiggle
about while we unruck socks, struggle
with zips, but they're out in it now, arms flung wide,
rain tattooing their palms and their tongues,
wading in the lake on the gravel,
while we're back in the pantry mopping up,
bringing buckets and meat tins and cloths
to catch the grey drips that keep tracking
through the tiles when the wind's in the east
that I said I'd get someone to fix
I'm reminded by that tightness in your lips,
so I settle to the job, shift stuff
off the shelves, clear the floor, the veg rack,
dry pears, wipe the spatter off onions.
Then later when I'm calling them in
for lunch, I find them squatting in the drive,
our heavy spades flat out beside
a land they've drained with canals
that connect and are linked to a sea
with its shingle beach where space
lego figures stand waiting for a boat
to ground. Turning at my voice, they frown,
puzzled, as if they'd left me ages
before and can't make sense
of my English, my obsolete accent.

The Show

Two-faced, our front door:
the pattern on the outside
panels more ornate,
its sharp corners rounded.
The handles don't match
either. In the dim hall
an ordinary knob,
knuckled like a fist,
but fronting the street
a flash metal plate
with a lever to press
as if it were really
a latch. Honestly
the show we put on
for strangers is shameful
sometimes, so eager.
If we're going to live
here much longer, I vote
we change the front door.

The Marina

My mother's car till last year,
it's not going anywhere now,
jacked up on stacked logs on the tarmac,
a rear wheel chocked, so Tim
can work underneath. He's teaching
himself. With the help of the Haynes
manual and a good socket set,
he did it, dismantled the clutch.
That's it, in the garage, I take it,
by the new one still in its box.
I peer at it on the way past
for my bike, no idea how it works,
but Tim knows and will make it go
in due course. He's propped the exhaust
on one of the school-desk chairs
from the playroom laid on its side.
The casing's there waiting. The gear stick's
on the passenger seat with its bits.
Outside the back door, this gold
low mileage 1980 Marina's
rearing up, almost rampant, his.

The Flat-warming

Because it was only a nick on the foot
that hardly hurt, she just went on
piling up plates and glasses by the sink,
slightly anaesthetized by the drink,
because the party had been a success,
because it was new, her first-time flat,
and she couldn't face waking up to the mess
and if she felt lightheaded, why worry,
she was young and happy, tidying up,
so it wasn't odd not to notice the blood
spreading, pooling on the dark blue vinyl
for some time, and though she was shocked
she assumed it would stop, started
mopping it up, just a vein bleeding
in the side of her foot, surprising how much,
but because she knew not to make a fuss
and had given up Guides before First Aid
and never liked 'Sternum' her Biology teacher,
because it was miles too late for her mum,
and the phone was impossibly far away
anyway over the new grey carpet,
because she wouldn't give in, lie down,
because she was strong, too fit to faint,
and tall too, five foot nine or ten,
such a straight column, such a weight of blood
pressing through her, that she bled and bled
and it wouldn't, couldn't, didn't clot.

Thirst

Baking in a queue on the M6 this June
somewhere, nowhere, near Birmingham,
you came back to me, 23,
in a white towel, wet from the shower,
stepping out onto cold tiles striped
by shuttered light. Italy.
Our first hotel. I could probably track down
the name of the town, but who cares.
It's your skin on the tip of my tongue,
your earlobe that cool drop's hanging on.

Creeks

North beyond Clare the townships
spread out and contract, Yacka,
Stone Hut – a wide street with a store
and a Soldiers' Memorial Hall.
The wheat and the vines give way
to sheep, to scrub. The road runs straight
and featureless through the heat
except for a dip every now and then,
a bridge over rocks and grass
so parched it must think it's a path,
not what the signpost calls it: a creek
with a name, waiting for water
to run, if the rain ever comes.
Willochra, Wild Dog, Nectar, Spear:
words for whispering in your ear.

In the Aboriginal Cultures Gallery, Adelaide

'Pitaru' I learn
  translates as drought,
  the same word meaning
'a constant pounding';

not from the black
hammer of the sun
as I thought at once,
but from the work

it meant, the rock-
hard seeds, like acacia,
they had to gather
and somehow crack

to extract the kernel,
bitter, but just
nutritious enough
to keep them alive.

Near Williamstown, South Australia

As I turn down into this ride
between pines I'm startled to find
my father's shadow beside me –
the upper body bent forward,
his stride more hesitant, stiffer
since the sciatica. Walking
in the sun together we raise
butterflies, yellow, too flighty
to make out their markings. Strange
bird calls, but the birds won't show,
they keep their names to themselves.
Straight ahead though a tree stump stirs
and, through binoculars, pricks its ears,
turns to stare our way. We stop,
spot another one, three, four, more
grazing. My father's not breathing,
leaning forward, the glasses held
steady now: his first kangaroos.

Living the Silence

Might be something to do with God –
what a Trappist aspires to perhaps
or the habit of holding your tongue
and listening, a Quaker meeting.

But there, in those stubborn parishes
with their thin farms, it's the term
used to describe how some couples
cope with indissoluble marriage.

Awkward Things

Cutting the finger-nails on my right hand
Introducing her, not remembering her name
Another appeal in the post from Greenpeace
A fly in the kitchen
Lust and lack of it
Johnny Baker muttering outside Mace
The conversation at the next table
How Kay would like to walk faster and farther

Take Two

Re-run that chill October evening, sevenish, the house a black box.
Let her swish into the drive, come to a stop, switch off.
Watch her heave her case from the car, feel about in her bag for the door key.
Stand outside as the lights go on, chart her progress from room to room.
Listen to the stairs flex under her, water running, the boiler igniting.
The heater glows orange on the bathroom wall, her breath films the mirror.
She washes and changes, buckles her watch back, checks the time.
She leafs through the letters stacked in the hall, drops them unopened.
The fridge light discovers her lips compressed, her arching nostrils.
There's bacon, she finds, a chicken carcass under foil, enough salad.
She fills the kettle and clicks it on, tips rice into the cracked blue mug.
She reaches for the phone and dials the office. She's standing very still.

I go back to that moment. We're leaving together, slipping on coats.
I'm thinking of the lift, how close it is, the glittering street.
I'm slow to react to the phone. I grimace, turn back. And this time I hear her.
The relief, the hope, not just the reproach, in her careful unlooked-for voice.
She's putting on the rice, the water's boiled. In twenty minutes I'll be home.
The wine will be warming, the pilaff cooked.

On His Own

Not tofu and cashews or what was left
of the aubergine bake heated up,
but his find on the bottom shelf
in Mace that he'd promised himself
the next time she took herself off
overnight to their daughter's. Fray Bentos
steak and kidney pie in that same
shallow tin. When the oven was hot
he sliced off the lid, slid it in
and was waiting for the pastry to crisp
and puff up, for some whiff of a life
that once was just his, when she called
from the hall, the arrangements had changed.

This Morning

cast bronze, twice life size,
I stood on the cliff looking down
at the crawl of the waves, their agitation,
container ships mere specks,
and when you complained of the cold
wind, could we move, I smiled
to myself and led the way home.

But this afternoon I'm the dusty
green plastic Hulk, free with Shreddies,
lying face down in the ashtray
with a couple of jaundiced curtain hooks
we know will never come in.

Past Talking

At the end of the day it's a job
loading the bikes on the carrier,
adjusting my pedal to slot
under the bumper, then hoisting
your heavy frame high enough
for the straight handlebars not
to catch on my saddle and twist.

They don't naturally fit together,
my light-weight tourer with its new
dynamo, its panniers – and the sturdy
lady's Triumph you've been riding
for thirty-five years, with its rusty
chain-guard, the Sturmey Archer
three-speed gears and the basket.

Contradictory, they need a good shove
sometimes to make them lie snug,
and a light touch to coax the crabs
through the spokes. We drive carefully off,
glancing back, checking, but soon
give them no more thought than a pair
of horses nose to tail in some field.

Visitors

Towards the end weakening
she'd let them in
to perch on the sofa
opposite him
and make conversation.
Just for ten minutes.

After they'd touched him –
by then his skin
was translucent – and gone,
he'd laughed a little
relieved by another
good deed done.

Lapse

No answer from the flat on the corner
of Amistad and Calle Mayor
so you climb the white road up the hill
past the terrace with the low goals for handball
and a sports centre built since your time.
At the top you turn away from the Chalet,
where someone may remember you still
in his prayers, and via the short cut
by the bins behind the Art Room
you slip into Languages. You listen
at the English office door and, hearing
nothing, you knock and go in. It's him
all right, marking, looking up
from the desk, a London bus
like a thought bubble over his head
and on a shelf a marble statuette
of the Virgin Mary, arms open.
He's wearing that shiny black blazer
with the silver buttons you'd forgotten
and a tie – of course – the blue diamonds.
Good day he says, *how can I help you?*
in Spanish, using Vd., not tú,
and you see that he hasn't a clue,
that he can't possibly imagine
turning into you, and your smile
stiffens, it's pathetic, you're hurt,
and, leaving the comfort you thought
you'd bring him from England unspoken,
you turn on your heel, let him stew.

Identity Parade

Hopeful of finding my penis
I work my way down the line,
taking my time as advised,
but gradually growing less
confident, more perplexed
by how alike they all look:
bell-pulls that ring no bell,
surreal pokers gone soft.
Might this one be mine
with its bulge of blue vein
or that one, shrunk by the cold,
skin concertinaed, a whiff
under the soap? Though the angle's
all wrong, perhaps my hand
would remember, could tell
if I'm warm. Tentative
I reach out, but freeze,
startled by the crazed
leathery back of my hand.

Old School Tie

Met him first I thought at Pete's fortieth
and we got on well. But he knew me
from school it turned out,
four or five years junior to me,
the headboy he'd hated faithfully
ever since for some offence
or maybe just for the way I'd looked,
he couldn't remember, but told me how
on a Sunday evening last September
chugging home into the cut
against an offshore wind and looming
banks of mud and cumulonimbus,
he passed me crouching in the stern
of the Enterprise as it drifted backwards,
yanking madly away at the outboard
that wouldn't catch. Made his day.

Travelling with St Thèrese

I missed her by a day in Fremantle.
I read it in the paper: she was coming
to the church of Our Lady of Mount Carmel
on the corner of Collick and Laidlaw
and staying two days. There were special
arrangements for parking, the hours
it was open, a number to phone.
One stage in her three-month tour
of Australia. For the detailed
itinerary the article referred
readers to her website. Apparently
she'd visited twenty-three countries
in the last seven years. Energy
I remembered she taught is the crucial
virtue in the struggle to be holy.
So no rest for her bones or whatever
remains of her are still flying round
the world a good hundred years
since she died. But with only four days
for the wheat belt, the karris, Margaret River,
it never for a moment crossed my mind
to hang on. After lunch we drove east
in our Hertz automatic as planned,
only turning back once – for water
melons chalked on a sign flashing past
that Kay glimpsed and fancied. The murmur
of the Fiat distanced me from the relic
of her hope that one day I may come
to love: like the child abandoning itself
without fear in its father's arms.

A Meeting

In the lift going up the child
inside me stays quiet, he likes it:
the speed we rise with, the light
that counts out each floor till we come
to a teetering stop and the doors
open by themselves. The child
wants to do it again, but the chief
executive's expecting me, yes,
take a seat, a minute to remind
myself why I'm here, to check
my list of objectives, tactics,
but the child can't care less, he's cross
to be made to wait, fidgets, wriggles
till I let him get down. What harm
can he come to or do, running about
in reception? The marble and glass
clatter with the racket, but the girl's
miles away at her screen and ignores
how he calls me to look, look, look
at his best forward roll that skews off
her plush strip of carpet, at his cartwheel
falling flat, the bang on his knee
I'm stroking as we stand at the window,
distracted by our raindrop races,
an ambulance flashing down below.

Close

Over these last few days
of black ice, iron frost,
of Tim going in and out
packing, hardly speaking,
I keep on finding myself
in that check-out queue again
behind them, my eyes resting
on the child on his mother's hip
sucking his thumb, half-asleep,
while the fingers of his other hand
twitch and nibble at her neck.
The woman, head turned away,
paying attention to her friend,
seems not to notice any more
than the glazed-eyed baby,
except that she hitches him up
and is holding him now, I'd guess,
just a little more closely.

Mending a Puncture

The boy's bent double in the garage,
he's hopeful, but the bike won't co-operate –
lying on its side, it jams its pedal
on the concrete so the wheel can't turn,
won't let him get at the valve.
The bike thinks it needs a new tyre.
It's bored with the boy's tight lips,
his feeble levering with the spoons,
his plucking at the inner tube,
and it can't believe how long
he's taking screwing the pump on.
With a faint hiss the tyre keeps deflating
as fast as he forces air in.
It's scornful of his panting, his sighs,
doesn't care what's happening in the house –
that the woman hardly ever comes out,
that the girl wears her walkman full time
and the yellow Allegro parks
elsewhere overnight now. The bike
just wants air in its tyres and oil
on its chain. It imagines itself
fizzing along in the slipstream
of a bus down the Brighton Road,
the shoppers stopping, mouths open,
the children in the passing cars pointing
and laughing. At Chessington Zoo
the queuing crowds let out a roar.
Growing stronger by the mile, the bike's
leaving Leatherhead behind, going on
past Box Hill, not planning to return –
it can't stand the mess the boy's making
with the glue, how he won't give up.

Permission to Breathe

It wasn't easy. He was still flying
missions then, navigating the Lancaster
accurately into the flak, into the foul-mouthed
shafts of the searchlights. Fifteen shaken minutes
from the aerodrome through the thin November dawn
on his motorbike and he was home. She was up
already with Tim in the scullery
putting the nappies to boil in the bucket.
Only one, the only one, he wouldn't be held,
stiffened against him, struggled and wailed.
It was tiredness, he told himself, tiredness and cold
that had set the tic going again in his eyelid.
Tilted by the child, she poured him stewed tea
and he took it to bed, warming his hands
a little round the thick white china.
Later aware of a murmur in the hall
he guessed she was strapping him in, manoeuvring
the pram, and he drifted off as silence settled.
At the Co-op she collected the butter ration,
at Willis' pig's liver for their tea,
and then she came home the long way round
beside the motionless cloudy canal
where only a mallard made v's on the water.
Tim fell asleep as they reached the gate
and suddenly limp from the broken nights
she flopped down by dad in the blacked-out room.
In that half hour before Tim whimpered
I began, though I was nothing to them.
As they slid apart, one of next door's hens
started clucking and mum almost tasted new laid
eggs for lunch – she'd ask Betty – but dad couldn't take
his eyes off the barrage pounding up
as they came in low for their final drop.

Old Money

He changed my five
sixpences
for half a crown,
assumed I'd love
his bright idea,
its weight and size.
He smiled above
my doubts, held out
his open hand
and pocketed
my jingling five,
my perfect pile,
those spiral stairs.
The single coin
he pressed on me
was useless, gross,
it made me cry,
so, in the end,
he swopped them back,
shaking his head
making a face
that to my shame
though he's long dead
I don't forget.

The Pain on His Face

Mum put her knitting down and Dad
leant forward in the big armchair
and actually cheered, the news
we were watching, in black and white:
a barrier it had taken an Englishman
to break through. And teamwork too. Brasher
set the pace for the first two laps,
Chataway replaced him and led till the bell
when Bannister went past and, somehow,
powered by the roar, accelerated,
fifty yards clear at the tape.
3 minutes 59.4 seconds.
I re-ran his day again and again:
the dispiriting rain and high winds first thing,
yet how undeterred he did his ward round
and sharpened his spikes, applied graphite
to stop the grit from the cinders sticking
and slowing him down, even so slightly;
how his legs buckled under him afterwards
as he blacked out, and they hauled him up,
hooked his arms round their necks and held him
for the camera, the pain on his face
speaking to me from by far the neatest
page in my scrapbook. Less eloquent was Dad
pinned in the doorway by Budapest,
men throwing stones at the Russian tanks,
their appeal to the west repeatedly broadcast
in broken English, till transmission stopped.
And as for our troops filing up the gang-plank,
coming home from Suez – the grinning asses –
he switched them off.

Getting On

This morning I was tipping out tea leaves
on the compost heap in a hurry
to get in, to wash up, to get on,
when through the falling blossom
our cream Zephyr six coasted in
and came to a stop. It was Dad
in his shirtsleeves who swung
open the door and climbed out
easily, younger than me.
Old man he said, cupping his hand
on my shoulder, *coming for a spin?*

The Lawnmower

Irreproachable, the racket of the Qualcast
coming and going in the cool
of the evening, every so often
running on the spot while he empties
the grass box. This is the man
we've given up kneeling in the window
watching the gate for. So intent
on his stripes that he looks straight through
our headstands, our new backwards skipping.
Though the motor's died, the blades
don't stop at once. We keep back,
do as we're told, don't touch.
It must be overgrown now, the grave.